Positive Parenting Guides: Parents' Guide to teaching Values to the Kids

Tommy R. Diaz

Terms and Conditions

Lawful Notification

The Distributor has strived to be pretty much as exact and finished as conceivable in the production of this report, despite the way that he doesn't warrant or address whenever that the items inside are precise because of the quickly changing nature of the Internet. While all endeavors have been made to check data given in this distribution, the Distributor takes care of mistakes, oversights, or on the other hand, the opposite translation of the topic in this. Any apparent insults of explicit people, people groups, or associations are inadvertent.

In viable exhortation books, similar to whatever else throughout everyday life, there are no certifications of payment made. Perusers are forewarned to answer on their

judgment about their singular conditions to in like manner act.
This book isn't expected to be used as a wellspring of legitimate business, bookkeeping, or monetary guidance. All perusers are educated to look for administrations with capable experts in lawful, business, bookkeeping, and money fields.
You are urged to print this book for simple reading.

Table of contents

Chapter 1

Chapter 2

Chapter 3

Chapter 4

Chapter 5

Chapter 6

Wrapping Up

r

Chapter 1

Morality lesson

As expressed previously, you genuinely must impart a positive arrangement of ethics and values to your kid on the off chance that you believe they should find success and be cheerful later on.
Numerous things in life will be significantly more challenging to achieve without legitimate qualities, on the off chance that they should be possible by any stretch of the imagination.

Positive relationships will be a lot simpler to work with legitimate virtues because your youngster will be more disposed to act in some positive ways. Achievement will likewise be accomplished a lot more straightforwardly for an individual with solid qualities contrasted with one who doesn't. This is because the kid with values will probably have a greatly improved set of instruments to utilize while making significant decisions. As you can see, virtues are vital for the improvement of your kid. For that reason, it ought to be exceptionally high on your rundown of needs and you ought to start showing them these qualities right away. Before you can start showing your kid ethics and their significance, you should first comprehend the basics.

The following section will get in contact with the basics of ethics and their significance for your youngster and the positive results that showing these qualities to your kid will most likely acquire what's in store.

The Basics

Ethics and values can be shown in various ways. Much of the time, what works for one

parent and kid will probably not produce something very similar
to the results of an alternate parent and kid. You need to investigate and attempt various methodologies. If something doesn't work the time has come to have a go at something different. There will be a great deal of experimentation with regards to bringing up your youngster. You should keep in mind that no one is great and this incorporates guardians.

It might be hard to keep searching for replies to assist you with breaking through to your kid, yet it is vital.
Your kid relies upon you for direction throughout everyday life. There are things you should do to ensure that they can satisfy their maximum capacity later on. There are many advantages to imparting a positive arrangement of ethics and values to your youngster.

Coming up next are a few instances of the positive advantages that your kid can get from having great ethics and values:

Self-Respect: If your kid is raised with a positive arrangement of ethics and values they will certainly grow up to have sound degrees of self-respect and self-worth. This is because a youngster who has positive ethics will settle on significantly more certain choices than a not. kid. These positive choices add up and the kid will realize that they use sound judgment and that they are a great individual. Self-respect contributes an incredible arrangement to the outcome of a youngster.

Experience in School:
Your kid will most certainly have a superior experience while going to class on the off chance that they have great ethics. They will be more liable for their activities and make an effort not to fault others for the things they foul up. Their educators will believe

them more and will be more ready to work with them.
You will see that a ton of children with great ethics like going to class since they figure out the significance of it.

Relationships:
At the point when your kid arrives at the age that it is the ideal opportunity for them to begin framing relationships, it will be a lot more straightforward for them to work assuming they have a decent set of ethics. Individuals will be significantly more learned to be around an individual that has a superior arrangement of ethics and values than a not. individual.

This is because individuals find it challenging to entrust an individual with unfortunate qualities and
ethics and trust are required in any relationship, whether individual or expert.

Finding a place with different
representatives will be truly challenging and
the main individuals
they will find who acknowledge them will
probably be others with unfortunate ethics.
Finding more individuals with unfortunate
ethics will simply bring down their ethics
even more and build up their perspective.
Then again, assuming you impart positive
ethics and values into your kid will draw
others into their life who have similar
arrangements of convictions.
They will see a lot better relationships and
will have numerous entryways of chance
open up for them. Great brings great and
awful brings terrible so it is vital to assist
your kid with being the best individual they
can be.

Accountability:
Youngsters who have great ethics are
generally substantially more responsible
than the people who don't. To that end, the
people who were raised with great ethics are

cut off from having much better friendships and amazing open doors throughout are everyday life forms of fault, rather they acknowledge when they misunderstand entirely followed through with something, and attempt to effectively transform it. This will likewise prompt considerably more trust between a parent and a youngster which is dependably good for a family relationship. This will make it more straightforward for your kid to converse with you, regardless of what is at the forefront of their thoughts, regardless of whether it implies that they need to admit to something they have done.

Chapter 2

Be the best example

Your youngster's psyche can be considered wiped. Everything around it gets absorbed. For that reason, it is vital to ensure that your youngster has a positive impact on their day-to-day existence. There ought to be one principal good example and anyway that is your occupation as a parent.

Understanding that your child is significant fosters a lot of their behaviors from what they see you do. It's as the platitude goes, "monkey see monkey do".
You want to ensure that you are continually setting a positive example for your kid. Your kid imagines that you are a hero and that you know the correct method for doing everything, which is the reason you should carry on like a super legend and forever be positive.

The accompanying section will reveal some insight into the significance of being a genuine example as a parent and the manners by which you can do such.

Be a Hero

As referenced above, you genuinely must carry on like a superhuman around your kid. I don't imply that you want to go out around evening time in a veil and cape and go out and battle furnished crooks. I imply that you want to continuously make the best decision in each circumstance, regardless of how troublesome it could be or what compensation an adverse choice might offer you. By doing this you will show your youngster that it is essential to constantly make the best decision.
You must show others how it's done. Almost certainly, your kid will get on the lessons being given when they are by example and not simply from things that you say. This is particularly obvious when guardians

make an effort to avoid something because it is terrible. You should comprehend that it is challenging for a kid to make sense of this idea. For example, many guardians tell their kids not to smoke cigarettes because they are unfortunate and can kill them, while the whole time they have a lit cigarette hanging out of their mouth, This message will not be held as the kid will barely care about it in the wake of watching their folks do precisely the exact thing they were telling them not to. The equivalent goes for showing your kid ethics; you should try to do what you say others should do!

You want to figure out what ethics you want to show your kid and find ways that you can exhibit these ethics by example. For example, if you maintain that your kid should figure out how to be thoughtful, you might assist a senior neighbor with conveying their food or assist them with managing their yard at no charge. Another way you can show this virtue is to provide

for a cause or give dinner to somebody out of luck. To show your kid being responsible you genuinely must assume a sense of ownership with all that is your shortcoming, regardless of how little you might think the issue is or how terrible the result might be. This will show your youngster to not fear the outcomes of telling the truth and to be more responsible for their choices throughout everyday life. If you
believe your kid should learn liability you might need to take a stab at taking them to work with you for a day so they can see every one of the obligations that you have consistently.

You may likewise need to sit down to chat with them about the obligations in the existence of taking care of the bills and ensuring that there is continuous food on the table. This will assist them with the understanding that life isn't one major game and will set them up for the day that they should become answerable for their own life. Fundamentally, what you want to do is figure out which virtues your kid might be missing or which ethics you might want to change about your kid

Furthermore, make a blueprint. Your endeavors may not work first and may set aside some margin to show progress however you will unquestionably find success in your endeavors

assuming you invest sufficient effort. Quite possibly the main thing you want to do is dissect your ethics and values and ensure you are displaying positive lessons as a parent.

Chapter 3

Begin Educating Youthful

You genuinely mustn't hold on until the later phases of a kid's life to begin showing them certain ethics and values and how significant they are to live. This is something that should be finished as quickly as time permits. You might feel that your kid is excessively youthful to grasp lessons about ethics. What's more, esteems, this isn't accurate. Youngsters see considerably more than many individuals naturally suspect they do and begin holding data from an early age.

Begin showing your kid the significance of ethics and values at an early age. Your endeavors will be significantly more beneficial if you do such.
The accompanying part will go over the significance of beginning to show your kid

ethics, youthfulness, and a few manners by which to do such.

The Sooner the Better

Many guardians wrongly hold on until a youngster's later stages in the improvement cycle before they make a move on the ethical guidelines of their kid. This is a serious mix-up and I will let you know why. By the time a kid is in the later phases of their advancement they now
have their very own psyche. It is a lot harder to shape a youngster's mindset when they are more established.
The more they develop the more through and through freedom they gain. They will ultimately reach a place where they would rather not pay attention to what you need to say and would prefer to settle on their own choices and get familiar with their lessons throughout everyday life. This can have exceptionally adverse results because the youngster won't have any desire to pay

attention to somebody who knows things as a matter of fact and will probably pursue silly choices. If you start at an early age, your kid's cerebrum resembles a wipe, as referenced beforehand.

Logical examinations have shown that a lot of your youngster's improvement begins in the initial five years of their life. Presently do you see the reason why Starting showing your kid early is so significant?

There are numerous ways that you can show your kid positive ethics and values at an early age. A couple of examples are given below:

Give Them Obligations:

Furnish your youngster for certain obligations around the house. Lounging around sitting in front of the television or playing computer games the entire day will have no sure

effect on their ethics. Your kid must have obligations that they need to do consistently, regardless of whether they are little liabilities. Two or three examples might be tidying up their wrecks or making their bed in the first part of the day. You will probably be astounded by how much contrast these little obligations make in your kid's ethics.

Consider Them Responsible:
You should consider your kid responsible for their activities. You additionally need to comprehend that children will be kids. It is critical to track down a good arrangement between mercy and being severe. A few guardians let their kids pull off completely a lot with practically no kind of discipline. They attempt to be the youngster's companion and not their parent which prompts the kid to feel that there are no genuine ramifications for any of their activities throughout everyday life. This will have exceptionally adverse results for them and will probably lead to them not arriving at their maximum capacity throughout everyday life.

Then again, if you are too severe, you won't have a beneficial outcome for your kid either. They will probably begin to overlook you because they don't feel near you and will conceal things from you and lie to you because of the dread of discipline.

Trustworthiness is the Best Strategy:
Your youngster must comprehend at an early age that lying is never alright for any reason. Assuming your kid misleads you there
should be a discipline of some kind or another. Be cautious while choosing your technique for discipline however because you would rather not be too harsh on your kid.
Another thing that you might try not to do is engage in made-up stories. A creative mind is a certain something yet assuming that a youngster is making stories up to escape Something there is an issue that should be tended to.

Charitable effort:
The charitable effort is an incredible way for a youngster to advance vital ethics forever. Indeed, even at an early age, a few worker affiliations will permit kids to assist them with their humanitarian effort. An example that you may
need to consider would be your kid making sandwiches in a food drive for the destitute. Another example may be to serve food in a food kitchen on a vacation. This will help your youngster to see the value in what they have and not be avaricious with things throughout everyday life. It will likewise train your kid to be thoughtful and humane throughout everyday life and furnish them with the ability to adorers
than themselves.

Chapter 4

Focus on what your youngster is barraged with day to day

In the present society, there are many negative things overall that can adversely affect your youngster and their arrangement of ethics and values. Wherever you look there is something negative or rough going on. The roads are
loaded up with mayhem and the media is loaded up with viciousness. Music is loaded with disdain and computer games are brimming with drug use. How might you shield your kid from every one of the outer elements that you don't need affecting your kid?
The response is basic, you need to invest energy with them and focus on what is happening in their life.

The accompanying section will give you a few examples of what you ought to stay away from and what you ought to pay special attention to with your kid while attempting to impart great ethics and values into their life.

Reach out

Various things in life can adversely impact your youngster. The main thing you can do to assist your kid with staying away from these

adverse impacts are to engage in their life. You want to realize what is the deal with them and the kinds of circumstances and impacts that exist in their life. Your kid might cause it to appear to be in some cases like you are keeping an eye on them or not allowing them to experience their own life. You need to disregard this because you must be engaged with your kid's life. Coming up next are a few examples of things you should be mindful of and things you stay away from that your kid should foster Decena t arrangement of ethics and values:

Know Your Youngster's Companions: Youngsters can without much of a stretch be impacted by other kids. At times, a youngster will pay attention to another kid over a grown-up. For that reason, you as a parent really should know who your kids partner with. If your youngster has adverse impacts as companions, their ethical standing might be at peril. Regardless of whether our lady concurs with what someone, in particular,
is doing, they concur ultimately begins to take an interest at any rate because they needed to acquire the acknowledgment of interest to individuals, this is just human instinct. The more that your youngster participates in these exercises the less terrible they will feel about it. This will prompt changes in your youngster's ethics and values and things they used to believe were not alright out of nowhere. This could

incorporate medication use, lying, taking, or other negative behaviors.

Keep an eye Out For Specific Computer games:

Computer games are becoming progressively rough. On top of that, they are likewise beginning to advance medication and liquor use and other sorts of behaviors more

and the sky's the limit from there. The issue with a youngster messing around, for example, is that a kid can experience issues in distinguishing what is alright in a computer game and what is alright, in actuality.

This prompts kids to do a few exceptionally stunning things. There have been occurrences where kids have been truly harmed or have harmed or even killed other youngsters. At the point when they were inquired as to why they did what they did, they would answer that it was alright in their computer game and that they didn't feel that anybody would get injured. Circumstances, for example, happen much more than you presumably suspect. This is the primary motivation behind why there are evaluations on computer game covers. Guardians need to quit purchasing computer games that are intended for individuals ages 17+ for small kids. There is a motivation behind why those games have mature evaluations.

They are not implied for minds that can be shaped as simply as a kid. Guardians like to attempt to fault computer games for their youngster's activities yet they ought to truly be wondering why they got it for their kid in any case.

Music:

Very much like other types of media, music can either be beneficial for your kid's ethics or can be negative. As a rule, it is

negative. You should understand what sort of music your kid pays attention to. In years preceding iPads and iPhones, your kid would pay attention to the music on their sound system and you would be ready to hear what they were
paying attention to. In the present age, kids are continuously strolling around with headphones in and you have no clue about the thing they are paying attention to. Require a moment to request your kid who some of their #1 performers are and inquire as to whether you can pay attention to a portion of their music with them at some point.
You genuinely must inquire as to whether you can tune in with them and not all alone because this will tell your kid that you are intrigued and not simply attempting to get into their life.

Extra energy:
You additionally need to understand how your kid is doing their available energy. If

you are attempting to help your kid's ethical norms, it would be o
consider putting your kid in a few extra-curricular exercises. These exercises will show your youngsters obligations on how to be responsible for their activities. This is vital for the improvement of a solid arrangement of ethics and values.

Chapter 5

Keep the line of correspondence open

It's vital that your kid feels as though they can converse with you about anything. This will elevate them, to tell the truth consistently and to be responsible for their activities. This is vital assuming you maintain that your kid should grow up to have areas of strength for a given virtue. Keeping an open line of correspondence with your kid will create numerous circumstances that will make the age in their future a lot more straightforward to adapt to and handle.

It is vital to remember that this may not generally be imaginable because you will in all likelihood hear things that you would rather not over the long run. You need to remain even-tempered as well as cool as a cucumber or this won't ever

help your youngster's morals. The following section will go over the benefits of opening up to your kid as well as certain difficulties you ought to be hoping to confront.

The Benefits of Being Open

Many benefits can be presented by opening up to your kid. You mustn't be specific with what you can be open
with your youngster about. Having conversations with your kid about issues they are confronting or things that they might be considering doing can give extraordinary open doors to you as a parent to ingrain ethics into them. Youngsters normally search for direction; it is how we as people work. Significantly, you positively offer that direction.

These conversations can offer numerous positive moral impacts to your kid. It will help them to be responsible for their activities. It will show them right
from wrong. It will show them adhering to their objectives. Quite possibly the main thing it will show them is to have

respectability and be straightforward regardless of what the results are.
You must be mindful of the way that you need to do half of the work in this cycle. You must be mindful of the way that
you will probably hear things that furious or frustrate you while you have an open relationship with your kid.
You should hold your head together on the off chance that you believe this cycle should work. If you can't fittingly respond to a circumstance, you are neither aiding your kid
nor provide them with a positive example of how to deal with their issues from now on.
Regardless of what you hear you need to move toward it with a clear mind. You need to remember and value the way that your kid is coming to you for direction. However much something infuriates you, you mustn't address your kid like you are distraught at them. You should show that you comprehend and keep in mind that you

don't need to like the conversation, you should respect them for coming to you. It will help this cycle enormously assuming you show your kid that they are building entrust with you by opening up to you. Give them somewhat more honors
or on the other hand let them do a couple of things you were unable to believe them to do before, for example, remaining out late with companions or getting the family vehicle.

Chapter 6

Search for chances to bring up great qualities and decisions

Assuming you believe your kid should grasp the worth or great ethics and all the benefits that they will bring to their life, you should call attention to the upside decisions that your youngster makes throughout everyday life. A few guardians commit the error of just bringing up the things that their youngster isn't doing accurately. This is an unfortunate behavior pattern and it is reasonable that they may not have the foggiest idea about another approach to nurturing, however they need to get familiar with another way quickly. You need to make no joking matter when your kid pursues the right choices throughout everyday life, particularly about important choices. This will support their behaviors and make them need to clutch the ethics that you have eaten about

them. The following part will meet up on the significance of bringing up the right choices your youngster makes as well as the positive ethics that their
character displays.

Bring up the Up-sides

Guiding out or focusing on only the negative things a kid does or some unacceptable choice that they make can be extremely harmful to their self-picture. This can put a kid at risk of losing their ethics and values and growing new ones that are negative rather than positive. Youngsters
normally look for their folk's endorsement so constantly zeroing in on a youngster's off-base doings can cause the kid to feel as though they are not a decent individual or are
not sufficient for you. You don't like your kid to feel as such as it will annihilate their future.

You want to build up each certain choice your kid makes with their life, regardless of how little of a choice it is. Emphatically supporting a behavior is a nearly ensured method for keeping that behavior proceeding. Whether it be that your kid got straight A's on their report card or chose to do their schoolwork before playing computer games, you want to ensure that you recognize it and ensure that they realize that you understand what they have done. You might need to set up a prize framework that is planned around building the ethical person of your youngster. For their more modest accomplishments along their excursion, you might offer them a little prize. At the point when your kid accomplishes a bigger objective ought to be blessed to receive a bigger prize. Remember, their prizes don't necessarily need to be material articles. Indeed, you might need to avoid compensating your kid with material articles however much as could be expected. Utilizing material items can regularly practice a kid create of expecting a prize each time they follow through with something. Rather offer rewards, for example, later bedtimes, companions remaining over, or permitting them to invest more energy on their computer game framework that day. The generally troublesome aspect in this is most probably the way that you need to figure out how to be adjusted. Similarly, as you can't zero in on the negatives of a kid, you can't zero in on the upsides either. Kids are, all things considered, just kids. They need direction and will pursue wrong choices every once in a while. You actually should consider your kid responsible for their activities and not rationalize them on the off chance that you believe they should have a decent arrangement of ethics and values. Whenever your kid does something wrong you want to call attention to it. Not exclusively will it be

beneficial for the ethics of your youngster it will likewise be
valued by your child. Children need to feel the structure. The structure is how you care for them. The way that you don't allow them to do anything they like shows that you love them, regardless of the way the structure behaves like it at that point. The main reality to remember while attempting to construct your kid's ethical norms is that you are the parent. You should have troublesome discussions and do troublesome things, yet it is supportive and benefits your kid.

For example, later bedtimes, companions remaining over, or permitting them to invest more energy in their computer game framework that day. The generally troublesome aspect in this is almost probably the way that you need to figure out how to be adjusted. Similarly, as you can't zero in on the negatives of a kid, you can't zero in on the upsides either. Youngsters are, all things considered, just kids.

They need direction and will go with the wrong choices now and again. You should consider your kid responsible for their activities and not rationalize them if you believe they should have a decent arrangement of ethics and values. Whenever your kid does something wrong you want to bring it up. Not exclusively will it be beneficial for the ethics of your kid it will likewise be valued by your child. Children need to feel the structure. The structure is how kids know that you care for them. The way that you don't allow them to do anything they like shows them that you love them, regardless of whether they carry on like it at that point. The main truth to remember while attempting to construct your kid's ethical principles is that you are the parent. You should have troublesome discussions and do troublesome things, yet it is in support of the benefit of your kid.

Wrapping Up

It is justifiable for you to check out at the errand of imparting a decent arrangement of values to your kid as a truly challenging excursion. Be that as it may, it truly needn't bother with being. By being a decent good example and being associated with your kid's life you will be doing a ton to guarantee that your kid grows up with a decent arrangement of values. Quite possibly the main thing you can do is essentially show your kid that you care about them and the significance of being a decent individual. You can do that, can't you?

The data that you have perused in this book ought to be exceptionally useful for you with regards to showing your kid's ethics and values. Simply apply what you have realized

and you ought to begin to see enhancements in
their personality in a matter of moments by any means.
I thank you for your time and I want to believe that you partook in this book. Best of luck!

www.ingramcontent.com/pod-product-compliance
Lightning Source LLC
LaVergne TN
LVHW052108160826
845678LV00015B/3426

* 9 7 9 8 3 5 5 0 0 4 1 1 8 *